BELIEFS AND CULTURES

Christian

Carol Watson

W
FRANKLIN WATTS
LONDON · NEW YORK · SYDNEY

© 1996 Franklin Watts

Franklin Watts
96 Leonard Street
London
EC2A 4RH

Franklin Watts Australia
14 Mars Road
Lane Cove
NSW 2066

ISBN: 0 7496 2368 3

Dewey Decimal Classification Number 230

A CIP catalogue record for this bbok is available
from the British Library.

Series Editor: Sarah Ridley
Designer: Liz Black
Consultants: Paul and Angela Helm
Illustrators: Belinda Evans pgs 10-11; Aziz Khan
pg 4 and pg 31.
Picture Researcher: Sarah Moule
Photographer (activities): Peter Millard
With thanks to Nabil Shehadi, Sherry Robinette
and Rev. Richard Adfield.

Photographs: Andes Press Agency 22t, 22b, 28, 29tl;
Bridgeman Art Library/(Galleria degli Uffizi, Florence)
4b, (Giraudon) 5, (Courtauld Institute Galleries) 6,
(Museo Poldi Pezzoli, Milan) 13b, (Prado, Madrid)
15t, (Private Collection) 17tr, (Siena Cathedral) 24;
Circa Photo Library 16b; Eye Ubiquitous cover (insert
left), 9, 18tl, 18tr, 20, 27tr; Robert Harding Picture
Library 8t, 13t; Hutchison Library 8b, 15b, 17tl, 26,
30b; Impact Photos cover (insert right), 14t, 27tl;
Magnum 12b, 16t, 17b, 30t; Panos 29br; TRIP 14b,
27b; with thanks to Van Poole's for the background
cover transparency; ZEFA 19t.
Printed in Great Britain.

CONTENTS

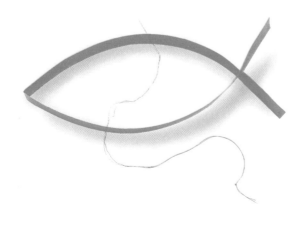

A Christian is someone who believes that Jesus Christ is the Son of God, who came into the world to save all people from their sins and show them the way to God. (A sin is something people do that is unloving and against God's laws.) Christians believe that if people are sorry for their sins, God forgives them and offers them a new life with him in this world and also in heaven after they have died. The word 'Christ' means 'anointed one' or 'Messiah'. Christians believe that Jesus is the Messiah or 'saviour' that God promised to the Jewish people.

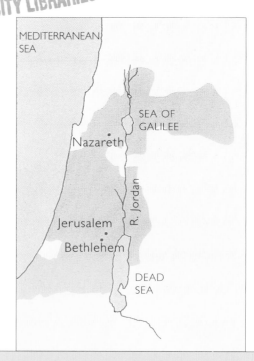

Jesus was born in Bethlehem, brought up in Nazareth, and during his ministry, travelled all around Galilee.

Here, the Angel Gabriel visits Mary to tell her she will bear the Son of God.

WHO WAS JESUS?

Jesus was a Jew and was born in Bethlehem in modern Palestine around 4BC. His human parents were called Mary and Joseph and were descendants of the Jewish King David. Before Mary married Joseph, an angel of God appeared to her and told Mary that she was going to have a child who was the Son of God. She was to name him Jesus. God had chosen Mary because she was obedient and pure. Jesus grew up in Nazareth and worked as a carpenter until it was time to do God's work.

THE TEACHINGS OF JESUS

When he was thirty years old, Jesus began to teach people about God. He chose twelve followers or 'disciples' (later called 'the apostles') and travelled around Palestine healing the sick, performing miracles and telling people how God wanted them to live. Thousands flocked to listen to his preaching. Jesus gave them two commandments: they were to love God with all their heart, soul, mind and strength, and they were to love each other as they loved themselves.

WHAT HAPPENED TO JESUS?

Jesus' teaching went against some of the beliefs of the Jewish high priests. They encouraged the Roman authorities to arrest him. Jesus was put to death by 'crucifixion'. This was an agonising death where the victim was nailed to a wooden cross and left to die slowly in the hot sun.

Three days after his death Jesus rose from the dead. This is called the 'resurrection'. He then appeared to his disciples numerous times over a period of forty days. Before he returned to be with God, his Father in heaven, Jesus commanded his disciples to carry on his teaching throughout the world. Jesus told his followers that although they could not see him he would always be with them, and that one day he would return again to judge the world.

The cross or crucifix has become a symbol to Christians of the suffering of Jesus Christ.

After Jesus had gone to be with his Father in heaven, God sent the Holy Spirit to guide and strengthen Jesus' followers. (The Holy Spirit is God at work in the world, helping people to be more like Jesus.) The disciples began to baptise, preach and heal the sick, just as Jesus had done. Thousands listened to them and became followers of 'the Way'.

The leaders of the Jews were afraid that these people might convert others, so they set out to persecute and kill them. One of the ringleaders, Saul, travelled far and wide persecuting Jesus' disciples. Then, one day Saul had a miraculous conversion. Instead of persecuting Jesus' followers, he changed his name to Paul and became one of the greatest Christian missionaries of all time.

Followers of 'the Way', or Jesus Christ, became known as 'Christians'. Christianity spread to the Mediterranean countries, including Greece and Rome. But the Ancient Romans persecuted the Christians and they were forced to meet and worship in secret.

The Conversion of St Paul by Rubens shows Saul blinded by a vision of Jesus.

The persecuted Christians had a silent secret code. To check if someone they met was also a Christian they drew half a fish in the sand. If the other person completed the fish they knew he was a believer, too.

Under the fish symbol, Christians wrote the Greek letters - I X Θ Y Σ (fish). We write this in English as ICTHUS. But the letters also stood for:

I	Jesus
X	Christ
Θ	God's
Y	Son
Σ	Saviour

MAKE A FISH MOBILE

WHAT TO DO:

1 Cut a strip of card 60cm long and 3cm wide, and fold the strip in half exactly. Press the fold.

2 Mark points 6cm from the two open ends. Draw a line 1.5cm downwards at one end, and 1.5cm upwards at the other end. Carefully snip where you have marked.

3 Slot the two open ends together to make your fish and tail.

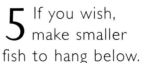

4 Measure 10cm inwards from where the paper crosses. Working with your cotton double, push the needle up through the top strip at the place marked. Make sure your cotton has a knot at the end.

5 If you wish, make smaller fish to hang below.

7

This Greek bible is open in position, so the word of God can be read to worshippers.

Christians believe that the Holy Bible is the written word of God. It is a collection of sixty-six books which include history, drama, poetry, letters, laws and stories of people's lives. There are two main sections in the Bible - the Old Testament and the New Testament. The word 'testament' means an agreement or promise.

THE OLD TESTAMENT

This tells the story of the creation of the world, and of God's promise to Abraham and his descendants, the Jewish people. This promise was that if they obeyed and trusted in him, and kept his laws, he would always love and protect them. Even when his people disobeyed his rules, God showed that he was a loving Father by giving them more chances to change their ways and turn back to him. The Old Testament was written down on scrolls in Hebrew by the scribes of ancient Israel.

The Dead Sea Scrolls, found here at Qumran, were copies of ancient Hebrew manuscripts of the Old Testament.

THE NEW TESTAMENT

This part of the Bible is about God's new promise. He sent his own Son, Jesus, into the world to offer forgiveness and a new life to all those who believe and trust in him. The New Testament tells of Jesus' life, his teaching and his healings. It ends with a prophecy of the future which tells us that Jesus will come again into the world. The New Testament was written in Greek by the followers that Jesus chose and trusted.

The Christian Church was built on the apostles' teaching. The New Testament is the record of what they taught. Jesus accepted the Old Testament as God's word. He himself said that he had not come to replace what the Jews believed in, but to fulfil it.

SPOTLIGHT

- The Greek Christians used to refer to the books of the bible as *ta biblia*, 'the books', so they became known as the Bible.
- The first full Bible in English was published in 1535.
- There is a Bible in every church building.
- The Bible has now been translated into nearly 2,000 languages.

This Christian family, like many others, reads the Bible together.

A BIBLE STORY - JESUS HEALS A PARALYSED MAN

On his travels Jesus visited a town called Capernaum. Many people came to hear him preach at the little house where he was staying. They filled the house and even gathered outside the door. There was no room for anyone to come near.

As Jesus was teaching, four men arrived at the house. Between them they were carrying a large mat, on which lay their sick friend. The man was paralysed and could not move. The friends realised it would be impossible to take the man through the door.

"Sorry lads, there's no room to get in there!" said one of the crowd. "Everyone wants to see Jesus," said another. "You'll have to wait your turn."

The four men were determined to reach Jesus somehow. They knew he would heal their sick friend. One of them noticed some steps leading up to the flat roof. "I've an idea!" he said. "Come on! Let's get him up there!"

So the men carefully carried the paralysed man on to the roof of the tiny house. Then, little by little, they dug a hole in the mud roof. When the hole was wide enough, the four men tied the ropes to the wooden structure supporting their friend's mat, and very gently, lowered him into the crowds gathered below.

"Look at that!" gasped some of the people.

When Jesus saw how much effort the four devoted friends had made to bring the sick man before him, he was moved by their faith. He looked at the man lying paralysed on the mat. Jesus knew that, apart from his illness, the sick man had other things that were troubling him, too. So he said quietly to the man, "Son, your sins are forgiven."

The religious leaders, who were among the crowd, looked horrified. "Who does this man think he is?" they thought. "Only God can forgive sins."

Jesus knew what they were thinking. "Why are you worried about the words I have just spoken?" he asked.

"You may not be able to see that I have the power to forgive sins, but you can see that I have the power to heal." Then Jesus turned to the sick man, "Get up!" he said. "Take your mat and go home."

The man who had been unable to move for so long leapt to his feet, picked up his mat and walked happily through the crowds. Everyone who saw this was astonished and praised God. They realised that if Jesus had the power to heal like this, perhaps he could forgive sins, too.

THE MAIN BRANCHES OF CHRISTIANITY

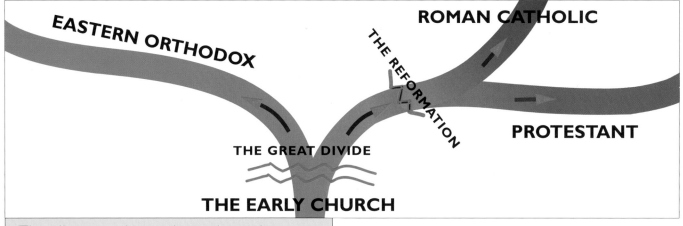

EASTERN ORTHODOX

ROMAN CATHOLIC

THE REFORMATION

PROTESTANT

THE GREAT DIVIDE

THE EARLY CHURCH

The diagram above shows how the Christian church has divided into three main branches since the time of Jesus.

The ancient Romans persecuted the Christians until the Roman Emperor, Constantine, became a Christian himself. In AD313 he issued a law called the Edict of Milan which stopped any more persecutions and allowed Christianity to be recognised officially. It eventually became the state religion and the huge empire of Rome was known as the Holy Roman Empire. Christianity spread west into other parts of Europe which were called Christendom.

The Pope is the head of the Roman Catholic Church and lives in Rome.

THE GREAT DIVIDE

In charge of the different regions of Christianity there were bishops or 'patriarchs'. Although they were supposed to have equal power, the Patriarch of Rome and the Patriarch of Constantinople (now Istanbul) were given more power than the others.

Greek Orthodox priests lead an Easter parade. Behind them people are carrying icons.

These two bishops had different ideas on how believers should worship, and eventually their arguments caused the Roman Church to break away. The Patriarch of Rome (later known as the Pope) became head of the Roman Catholic faith, with services conducted in Latin; and the main Orthodox Church was centred in Constantinople, with the services conducted in Greek.

THE REFORMATION

Throughout the Middle Ages, the Christian church continued to spread and change. People with strong beliefs began to challenge the Roman Catholic way of worship. One of these was a young German monk, called Martin Luther. He was shocked by the way some of the Roman

Catholic priests were behaving and thought the church had moved away from the teaching of Jesus.

PROTESTANTS

Martin Luther refused to submit to the authority of the Pope (the Patriarch of Rome). He and others 'protested' at the existing ways of teaching and worship, and set up their own form of Christianity. These rebels were known as Protestants. Their services were no longer in Latin, but were held in German, so the people of that country could understand what they were saying and hearing.

Martin Luther and his followers started the Protestant branch of Christianity.

WAYS OF WORSHIP

Christians meet together to worship God, to learn together and to celebrate their beliefs. They listen to passages read from the Bible, say prayers and sing hymns (songs of praise). Any group of Christians meeting together regularly is called 'a church'. Buildings where Christians meet are also called churches.

Inside a country church the vicar leads the congregation in worship.

Christians may worship together at any time, but the main day for worship is a Sunday. This is the Christian sabbath (day of rest and worship) because it is the day that Jesus rose from the dead. Church services are usually led by the vicar or priest. Some churches have organ music and choirs to accompany their music; others are less formal and have instrumental groups. Children sometimes go to classes before, during or after church services. These are called Sunday School.

Gospel singers sing praise songs (hymns) backed by a modern instrumental group.

THE LORD'S SUPPER

Before he was crucified, Jesus and the twelve disciples ate together for the last time. This is called 'The Last Supper'. At this meal Jesus passed around bread and a large cup of wine to his disciples, telling them that this represented his body and blood, which he was about to sacrifice for the sins of mankind. Jesus commanded his followers to remember him by celebrating this supper until he returns again to the world. All Christians do this in the celebration known as Mass, Holy Communion, the Eucharist or the Lord's Supper.

This painting of *The Last Supper* shows Jesus sharing the bread and the wine with his disciples.

Some Roman Catholics and Orthodox Christians celebrate Mass daily. In Protestant churches Holy Communion may be celebrated less frequently. It could be weekly, monthly or even twice a year.

During the Lord's Supper, the priest blesses the bread and wine before giving it to the congregation.

SPOTLIGHT

- Roman Catholics and Orthodox Christians believe that the consecrated bread and wine given to them by the priest at Mass actually become the body and blood of Jesus. This is called Transubstantiation.
- Protestants believe that the bread and wine are symbols of Jesus' body and blood.

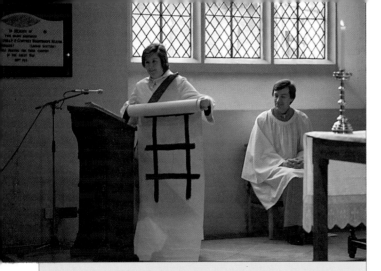

Vicars and priests wear special garments to show that they have been trained to work full time on God's behalf.

The Sacraments
- A sacrament is an 'outward and visible sign of an inner and spiritual grace'.

- Roman Catholics and Orthodox Christians recognise seven sacraments:
  * baptism,
  * confirmation,
  * the Lord's Supper,
  * penance,
  * extreme unction (anointing the sick and dying),
  * holy orders (bishops, priests and deacons)
  * marriage.

- Protestants recognise two sacraments:
  * baptism
  * the Lord's Supper.
  They believe these are the two commanded by Jesus.

Protestants, Roman Catholics and Orthodox Christians have other differences in their ways of worship. Protestants concentrate on hearing the word of God and obeying it. At their Sunday services the main part of the celebration is the sermon. This is a talk given by the vicar or preacher to the congregation which is based on readings from the Bible. Roman Catholics and Orthodox Christians have services which concentrate much more on worship and the Sacraments.

As well as celebrating the Lord's Supper much more frequently, Roman Catholics and Orthodox Christians go to Confession. There they privately tell the priest their wrongdoings and ask for forgiveness from God. If they have committed a serious sin they must receive the Sacrament of Penance before celebrating Mass.

A girl kneels to make her confession to the priest in the Confessional.

Roman Catholics often have statues of the Virgin Mary in their churches.

Orthodox Christians have portraits of saints, called 'icons' in their homes and churches.

Men and women of exceptional holiness officially recognised by the Christian Church are called 'saints'. The apostles, the Virgin Mary (mother of Jesus) and the martyrs (people who died for their faith) were the first saints. Roman Catholics and Orthodox Christians honour the saints and pray to them, especially the Virgin Mary. They also celebrate saints' days.

PRIVATE PRAYER

Christians also worship individually. They experience God and talk to him in private prayer as well as worshipping together.

A Christian woman kneels to pray quietly at home.

This country church perches on a hillside, its spire pointing to heaven and visible for miles around.

Sick people travel to Lourdes, in France, where for many years, miraculous healings have taken place.

Throughout history Christians have created beautiful buildings in which to worship God together. Sometimes these are very ornate with rich tapestries, statues and elaborate paintings. Others are plain and simple, built in peaceful countryside surrounded by the beauty of nature. The church is often the building that stands out the most in the community. But churches can be found anywhere. The building is not as important as the spirit and faith of the church members.

The entrance to a Christian church is often by the door facing west.

Opposite that door, at the east end of the church, is a table with a cross and candles, called the altar. In front of the altar (to either side) are the pulpit, from which the priest speaks, and the lectern which holds the Holy Bible. Many churches have beautiful stained-glass windows which show colourful scenes from Bible stories.

Some Christians choose to separate themselves from the world, give up all their possessions and devote their lives to worshipping God. The men become monks and live in monasteries; the women become nuns and live in convents.

MAKE A COLOURED CHURCH WINDOW

Chartres Cathedral in France is famous for its beautiful stained glass windows.

YOU WILL NEED:
- *thin black card or paper*
- *coloured tissue paper* • *glue stick*
- *scissors* • *white pencil*

WHAT TO DO:

1 Think about the design of your window. Draw the shapes you want to create on the back of the black card. Cut them out.

2 Tear or cut out different coloured pieces of tissue.

3 Using the glue, stick the tissue paper on the back of the card. Overlap it in places to create different effects.

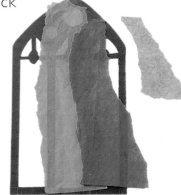

4 When you have finished, hang or stick the card against a window so the light can shine through.

CHRISTIAN FESTIVALS

Christian festivals are closely related to the life of Jesus. The main Holy Day (holiday) is the day of his birth. Protestants and Roman Catholics celebrate this on the 25th December, but Eastern Orthodox Christians celebrate it on 7th January. We do not know exactly the date that Jesus was born.

This Christian nativity scene shows Mary, Joseph and the baby Jesus in the manger.

ADVENT

This season begins four Sundays before Christmas. It is the time when Christians prepare for Christmas, the time of Jesus' birth. It is also a time when Christians look forward to Jesus' second coming, when Jesus will return to overcome evil and bring God's justice to the world.

CHRISTMAS

Christians celebrate Christmas because they commemorate the birth of Jesus Christ. They give each other presents because they remember God gave Jesus as a gift to the world. Jesus was born in a stable in the town of Bethlehem. The night of his birth angels of God appeared to local shepherds and told them that the 'Saviour', or Messiah, had been born. The shepherds went to find the baby Jesus and worshipped him. Meanwhile, far away in the East wise men, called astronomers, had been studying a new star in the sky. It meant that a new king had been born. They travelled for days to find the place where the star was. There they found Jesus. They worshipped him and gave him rich gifts of gold, frankincense and myrrh.

MAKING CHRISTMAS WRAPPING PAPER

YOU WILL NEED:

- some clean, medium-sized potatoes
- a chopping board
- a sharp knife
- a felt tip pen
- paint brush
- gold and silver poster paints
- newspaper
- large sheets of plain white and coloured tissue paper
- ♣ Ask an adult to help you with the cutting.

WHAT TO DO:

1 Cut a potato in half and draw a star on it with a pen.

3 Lay out a sheet of paper ready for printing. Paint the star shape gold or silver. Press firmly onto the paper.

2 Very carefully use the point of the knife to cut round the outline of the star. Then cut away the potato from the edge of the star, about 1cm deep.

4 The star design will print. Repeat as often as you want, experimenting with colour.

LENT

This is a period of forty days preparation for Easter. During Lent many Christians remember the time that Jesus spent in the desert fasting (going without food) and praying, before he began God's work. Some Christians give up eating their favourite food or drink in Lent in order to fast in some way. Lent is supposed to be a time of meditation and prayer.

The day before the beginning of Lent is called Shrove Tuesday. It has this name because it is the last day of Shrovetide. In the Middle Ages, Christians were called to church to

On Shrove Tuesday people make pancakes, 'tossing' them to turn them over.

be 'shriven' (confess their sins and ask for forgiveness) before Lent. Shrove Tuesday was the last day for feasting and eating up food before fasting in Lent. Eggs were among the forbidden foods of Lent and so were used up by making pancakes. Nowadays Shrove Tuesday is often known as Pancake Day.

The first day of Lent is called Ash Wednesday. In some churches on this day, the priest uses ash to make the sign of the cross on the forehead of each worshipper. This is to symbolise that they have repented of their sins and received forgiveness.

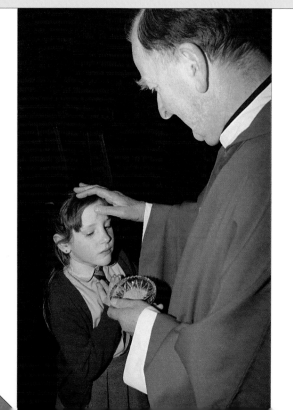

On Ash Wednesday, the priest makes the sign of the cross (in ash) on the head.

Making Pancakes

WHAT TO DO:

1 Put the flour and salt into a mixing bowl. Make a hollow in the centre and break the eggs into it.

2 Add half the milk and gradually draw in the flour with the spoon. Do this until the batter is smooth. Stir in the rest of the milk. Pour the mixture into a jug and leave to stand for an hour.

3 Then melt the butter in a frying pan and swill it round. When the fat is hot, pour in a thin layer of batter. Tilt the pan so that the batter covers the base.

4 Cook the pancake until bubbles appear and the edges turn brown. Flip the pancake over with a spatula and cook it on the other side.

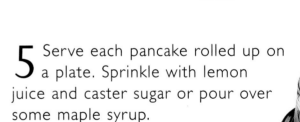

5 Serve each pancake rolled up on a plate. Sprinkle with lemon juice and caster sugar or pour over some maple syrup.

This medieval picture of the Crucifixion shows Jesus dying on the cross, with his mother, Mary, watching below.

HOLY WEEK

The week preceding Easter is called Holy Week. It begins with Palm Sunday, the day the crowds waved palms to welcome Jesus as he rode into Jerusalem on a donkey. The Last Supper is commemorated on Holy Thursday, sometimes called Maundy Thursday.

Good Friday

This is the day Christians remember the crucifixion of Jesus. The greatest sacrifice anyone can make is to die for someone else. Jesus died so that all people could receive forgiveness and have a relationship with God. As he was nailed to the cross dying, Jesus asked God to forgive those that were executing him. When he was dead, Jesus' body was taken to a tomb. There it was wrapped in cloth, and a huge stone was rolled across the entrance to the tomb. For Christians this is a day of fasting and sorrow. The name "Good" probably meant "God's" Friday, or possibly started at a time when the word "good" meant "holy."

Easter

Easter Sunday is a joyful celebration because it is the day of Jesus' resurrection and it is the most important festival for Christians. Three days after he died, Jesus rose from the dead and appeared to his followers. He showed that when our bodies die, it is not the end. There is an everlasting life with God for those that believe in him. On this day churches are decorated with flowers and Christians rejoice, sing, and give each other presents. Many people remember Easter day by giving each other Easter eggs. These are a symbol of the new and everlasting life that Jesus gave to all believers.

Decorating Easter Eggs

What to do:

1 Cover your work area with newspaper. Put each egg in a washable egg cup and paint all over with a bright color. Leave to dry.

2 When the eggs are dry choose different colors to paint patterns. These could be spots, stripes, or even faces.

3 Try out different effects. You could try using your own fingerprints to create an interesting design.

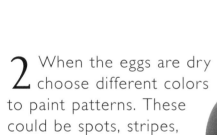

4 Use some colored tissue to line a small basket or bowl and fill it with your painted eggs.

The family unit is very important for Christians. A Christian couple tries to provide a secure and loving environment in which their children can grow up learning about God. Whenever an important Christian celebration takes place it is a time for relatives to join together and rejoice.

People watch as a woman is baptised in the river.

BAPTISM

The sacrament of baptism symbolises the washing away of sins and being born into a new life with Christ. Jesus himself was baptised in the River Jordan and told his followers to baptise others. So baptism has always been a sign of, and a way of, becoming a Christian.

At first, baptism was just for adults who had been prepared for it by learning about Christian beliefs. Baptism often took place in a river. The new Christians were dipped under the water and lifted up again as a sign of a new start in life. This is called 'immersion'. The custom of baptising babies started when Christian parents wanted their children to belong to Christ as soon as possible because they were being persecuted and dying for their faith. Many Roman Catholics believe that baptism is so important it must be carried out soon after birth.

Nowadays infant baptism is called a 'christening'. As babies cannot make the promises to follow Christ that are usual at baptism, they have godparents who do this on their behalf.

A Roman Catholic priest baptises a small baby, with his family gathered round.

Infant baptism takes place at the font. This contains the water which is sprinkled over the baby's forehead.

When the parents and godparents of the baby have made their promises, the priest sprinkles a little water (and sometimes oil) over the baby's forehead. He or she uses the baby's 'Christian' name and says, "I baptise you in the name of the Father, and of the son, and of the Holy Spirit". Then the priest makes the sign of the cross on the baby's forehead and everyone welcomes the child into the family of Christ.

CONFIRMATION

For some Christians this takes place when the child is old enough to understand the meaning of being baptised a Christian. The relatives and godparents of the child come to a special service in church sometimes attended by the local bishop. In front of the congregation, those being confirmed make the promises they were unable to make at baptism, 'confirming' their membership of the family of Christ. The bishop anoints the forehead with holy oil in the form of a cross. Roman Catholics and Orthodox Christians believe confirmation is a sacrament.

Girls often wear white dresses and boys wear trousers and white shirts at their own Confirmation service.

A Christian bride usually gets married in white, which is a symbol of purity.

MARRIAGE

The Bible says that marriage is a gift from God. It is God's purpose that a husband and wife should be united in love throughout their lives, just as Jesus Christ is united in love with his Church. Most Christians believe that marriage is a life-long commitment and that divorce is wrong. Roman Catholics are not allowed to re-marry if they divorce.

Christian couples are expected to prepare carefully for their new life together. Before the marriage service the priest or vicar will meet those intending to get married to give them advice and to make sure the couple realise the serious step they are taking. Christians get married in church with their relatives and friends around them to witness their vows.

INTERVIEW

Being a Christian helps our marriage work, because when we have problems or arguments we pray about them and ask God to help us forgive one another. God guides us through the bad times and keeps us together through all the ups and downs.

Jane Drew   age 43
Channel Islands

At the marriage ceremony (or wedding), the priest asks the couple to make solemn promises to the one they love, before God and with God's blessing. The congregation sing hymns, say prayers and celebrate the joyful occasion. Sometimes they also celebrate the Lord's Supper at the ceremony.

At a funeral service the coffin is lowered into the ground as the priest commits the person to God.

DEATH

Although it is a very sad time when a member of a family dies, for Christians it is also a time of thanksgiving and hope. Christians are comforted because they believe that the loved one who is no longer with them is now with Jesus and God. They believe that although the person's body is dead, the spirit of a Christian is in heaven, where there is no more pain or sadness.

A funeral service marks the end of a human life on earth. It is the opportunity for the friends and family of that person to express their grief and sorrow, to give thanks for the life which has ended in the world and hand that person into God's keeping. The church service can be short and quiet with a few prayers, or the relatives may want to fill the church with people and singing and have a talk and readings.

After the funeral service, the coffin containing the body is either buried in the ground or cremated. Before this happens the priest commits the person's spirit to God.

A faithful Christian looks forward to the time of their death being the time when they will leave for their true home with God.

These Rumanian women clean and decorate the gravestones of their relative.

Mother Teresa of Calcutta is a nun who came out of her convent in order to help the poor.

professions also try to do their job in the most 'Christian' way possible. This means that at all times they must be honest, trustworthy and caring, even if others order them to act differently. Many Christians do voluntary work to help the poor and underprivileged throughout the world. Wherever they are, and however they work, Christians pray to God to ask for guidance in the way they should behave and in the decisions they make.

The most important thing for all Christians is to love God and live their lives for his purpose. Christians aim to be as much like Jesus as possible, and care for other people around them. They try to use their God-given talents for the good of others and to spread the gospel of Jesus Christ.

Monks, nuns, priests, vicars and missionaries devote their lives to serving God and helping people. Christians who work in business, teaching, medicine and other

MISSIONARIES

Christians want everyone to be given the opportunity of having a new life with God. A Christian missionary is someone who travels to places where

Christians worship together in Kenya, East Africa.

people have never heard about Jesus, and tells them the things he taught. St Paul was the first Christian missionary, but since the time of the early Church there have been many missionaries who have spread Christianity throughout the world.

From the 2nd century there were Christian churches on the north coast of Africa because this was part of the Roman Empire. Hundreds of years later European traders and missionaries spread the faith to other parts of the African continent.

Today Christianity is spreading more in Africa than in Europe and North America.

In the 10th century, Greek monks spread Orthodox Christianity to Russia, and from the 16th century onwards Spanish and Portuguese soldiers and missionaries spread Roman Catholic Christianity to South America. In the 17th century the Pilgrim Fathers took Protestantism to North America, and over many years other missionaries have taken the faith to parts of Asia. There are now approximately 1,400 million Christians in the world.

This map shows all the areas in the world where Christianity is the main religion.

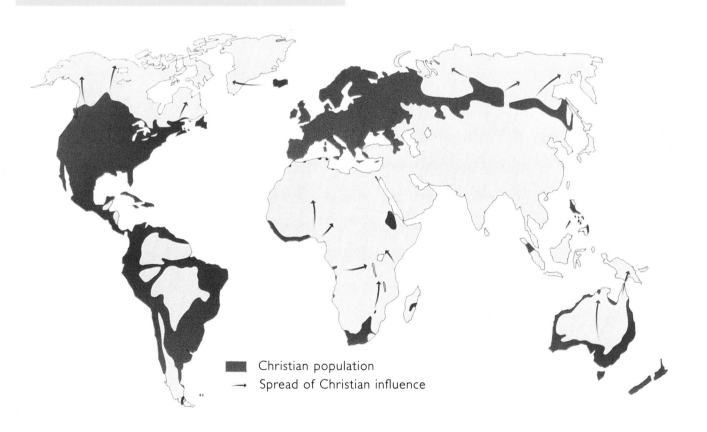

Christian population
→ Spread of Christian influence

GLOSSARY

angel servant and messenger of God.

apostle one of the twelve disciples chosen by Jesus to go out into the world and preach the gospel.

BC is short for Before Christ. About 500 years after Jesus lived, Christian scholars worked out a system for dating years counting from what they thought was the year of his birth. Later historians realised that Jesus was born four years earlier than had been recorded.

commandment an order, law or command.

crucifixion a very cruel way of putting someone to death, by nailing or binding them to a cross.

frankincense a strong smelling incense used in the East for burning in ceremonies.

Hebrew another word for Jew or the language of the Jews.

Messiah the leader or saviour that was promised to the Jewish people and foretold by the prophets of the Old Testament.

miracle something that happens that is beyond human power and understanding.

missionary someone who travels to different parts of the world to help people and tell them about God.

monks and nuns men or women who choose to give up any desire for wealth, success or marriage and go to live in religious communities (monasteries or convents) devoting their lives to the will of God.

myrrh a strong-smelling resin used in incense, perfume and medicine.

persecute to injure or harrass someone (usually because of what they believe in).

prophecy predict what is to come in the future (in the Bible, inspired by God).

pulpit a platform or raised box-like structure from which the priest speaks to the church congregation.

resurrection the act of rising from the dead.

scroll a roll of parchment or paper used for writing on in ancient times.

tomb a large cave-like hole made in rock or earth where a dead body is buried.

INDEX